HEROES AND WARRIORS

Charlemagne

FOUNDER OF THE HOLY ROMAN EMPIRE

BOB STEWART

Plates by JAMES FIELD

Firebird Books

First published in the UK 1988 by Firebird Books
P.O. Box 327, Poole, Dorset BH15 2RG

Copyright © 1988 Firebird Books Ltd
Text copyright © 1988 R.J. Stewart

Distributed in the United States by
Sterling Publishing Co, Inc
2 Park Avenue, New York, NY 10016

Distributed in Australia by
Capricorn Link (Australia) Pty Ltd
P.O. Box 665, Lane Cove, NSW 2066

British Library Cataloguing in Publication Data

Stewart, Bob
    Charlemagne : Founder of the Holy Roman
    Empire. — (Heroes and warriors).
    1. Charlemagne, *Emperor of the West*
    2. France — Kings and rulers — Biography
    I. Title II. Field, James III. Series
    940.1'4'0924   DC73

ISBN 1 85314 0058

Series editor Stuart Booth
Designed by Kathryn S.A. Booth
Typeset by Inforum Ltd, Portsmouth
Colour separations by Kingfisher Facsimile
Colour printed by Riverside Printing Co (Reading) Ltd
Printed and bound in Great Britain at the Bath Press

Charlemagne

FOUNDER OF THE HOLY ROMAN EMPIRE

Charlemagne as depicted in a late sixteenth-century engraving of the Song of Roland *in which he is described as the 'King with the grizzly beard'.*

THE CAROLINGIAN EMPIRE

Extensions to the Empire made by 814 AD
Kingdom of the Franks in 771 AD when the death of Carloman united the territories under Charlemagne
△ Abbeys, priories and convents

Charles the Great

The achievements of Charlemagne – Charles the Great – were vast and complex. Perhaps the most telling aspect of his rule is that within a generation of his death, he was as much the subject of legend as of factual history. The power and skill of this one man built the great Frankish empire, and upon his death seemingly it died. But only in the territorial and political sense, for during his reign was born the important concept of the Holy Roman Empire. Initially, the political manoeuverings of Pope Leo III created the concept of the Empire, when he crowned Charles in Rome on Christmas Day of the year A.D. 800. Yet the new role of emperor was held in control by Charles who used it for his own ends, which were often of the highest order and extended far beyond mere materialism. Upon his death, the concept was to develop into one of papal supremacy over the emperor, a tense relationship which affected the future history of Europe.

In this study of Charlemagne, the emphasis is mainly upon two major aspects of his life: his military campaigns and his development of a unified European culture. Though the second aspect was short-lived, it remained as an ideal concept that inspired future kings and emperors; and the first has hardly been surpassed by any superior achievement to this day.

The history of those achievements is complex. Charlemagne fought and worked on several fronts at any one time; in the military, political and cultural senses. Thus, a simple linear record of his life and rule is impossible and cannot be pinned down as a simplistic historical account. Any narrative of his life develops along several parallel routes. A typical example is the pattern of revolt displayed by the conquered Saxons in what is now modern Germany. For much of his reign they persistently took advantage of Charles' absence in Italy or Spain to revolt against his rule. To give even a simple account of this sequence demands chapters that travel back and forth between the various territories that Charles conquered and ruled. Thus there is a pattern not only of territorial movement and campaigning, but of interaction through time, politics and dynastic struggles. In other words, much of the story weaves in and

Charlemagne and one of his sons, from the Leges Barborum*, a tenth-century copy of a Carolingnian manuscript.*

out, sometimes travelling back in time, sometimes forwards, in order to achieve a practical overview of the struggles and triumphs of Charlemagne.

Of particular importance to understanding Charles' rule is the need for a clear picture of the geography and political divisions of the huge territories over which he ruled. Without this, one cannot begin to grasp the size and complexity of Charles' achievements – such as the uncanny speed with which he could move troops across great distances. For example, he moved his army from Italy to Saxony to surprise tribes in revolt, a distance that is still great today with modern transport; but this the Franks traversed at speed with an army mainly on foot, with horse support and a massive baggage train.

Yet Charles' cultural achievements are as remarkable as his troop movements and campaigns: he was a builder, a political governor, a religious propagandist, and a reformer and patron of the liberal arts and sciences. It is inevitable that much will be omitted in this study but the bibliography lists several larger and more detailed works on specific aspects of Charles and his effect upon European history and culture.

The Franks

The Franks, over whom Charlemagne came to reign in the year 768, were originally a loose confederation of Germanic tribes. By the sixth century they had begun to force their way into Gaul (France and Belgium), and there they eventually settled. The modern name of France comes from the word *frank*, though the characteristics of the early Franks were very far removed indeed from those of the modern French peoples.

The invading Franks, wielding their famous *franciscas*, or short-handled throwing axes, fought on foot. They ousted the Gallic landowners who were the last remnants of the Roman Empire, conquered the Visigoths in the south of France, and fought other Germanic tribes, such as the Burgundians and the Alamanni, who were already settled there.

The great Frankish leader who unified the confederacy into a powerful entity was Clovis, first of the Merovingian kings. These rulers were replaced several centuries later by the House of St Arnulf, the family line of Charlemagne.

Frankish ornaments found in German grave; purse frame (above left) and (below) plaque, sword hilt and brooch.

The Merovingian dynasty began as a vigorous force that firmly developed the Franks into a national entity, and made many conquests that extended Frankish territory. However, by the seventh century, the powerful blood of Clovis had been diluted considerably and King Sigibert III of the Merovings was a mere puppet under the control of his Mayor of the Palace. It was from these Mayors of the Palace – senior officers of the royal house – that Charlemagne's ancestors were eventually to become kings in their own right.

After further degeneration of the Merovings, and various attempts by ruthless Mayors to take full control of the kingdom, Pepin le Bref, the father of Charlemagne, was elected as King of the Franks in 752. Thus, within a period of about 300 years, the Franks had developed from a general confederacy of Germanic invaders with mere tribal links, into a fully-fledged kingdom. Furthermore, they had experienced the development and then degeneration of one major unifying royal line, the Merovings, and replaced this finally with a most vigorous governing family, the Arnulfings, who produced the great emperor Charlemagne.

System of Government

The Frankish system of rule was enlarged and refined under Charles, but was still very different from any system employed in modern history.

7

Examples of early Frankish costumes.

There was no uniform code of law, and very little in the way of legal redress for common folk wronged by their superiors. Ultimately, all laws and decisions stemmed from the king, whose decree or word was absolute. Charles saw the wisdom of maintaining local traditions of justice in the varied regions of his great realm, and gave instructions that cases should be heard according to regional laws.

But authority was vested in the nobility, who held their power from the emperor. The line of power ran from emperor to king (Charles' sons) to sub-king, to duke, to count. The system of counties was essential to Frankish government, and a count could wield considerable power, particularly in far-flung regions.

To maintain some overall supervision of the nobility and the enforcement of royal decrees, Charles kept his court mobile, although his favourite and main palace was at Aachen. The term 'palace' originally referred to the gathering around the king, rather than an actual building. However, even with his extensive travels and campaigns, Charles could not maintain personal supervision of everything and so he appointed travelling supervisors or commissioners, known as *missi dominici*. This system was formalised in the year 802, although it had been operational in early forms during the preceding years of his reign.

Although such travelling overseers had been occasionally employed by earlier Frankish kings, Charles was the first ruler to define and formalise their role fully. The *missi* were both priests and laymen; they were appointed for a term of one year in specified countships and complaints against count or bishop were brought before them. In theory the system was efficient and just; in practice it was prone to the limitations of travel, seasons, and the possibility of corruption, which was inevitable in such an extended empire.

Man and Emperor

We have clear descriptions of Charles from his chroniclers and contemporaries; he is probably the first powerful figure to emerge from the Dark Ages as a completely documented ruler.

He was tall and stoutly built . . . his height just seven times the length of his own foot. His head was round, his eyes large and lively, his nose somewhat above the common size, his expression bright and cheerful. Whether he stood or sat his form was full of dignity; the good proportion and grace of his body prevented the observer from noticing that his neck was rather short and his person rather too fleshy. His tread was firm, his aspect manly; his voice was clear but rather high pitched for so splendid a body. His health was excellent; only for the last four years of his life did he suffer from intermittent fever. To the very last he consulted his own common sense rather than the orders of his doctors whom he detested because they advised him to give up the roast meats that he loved.

(from the chronicler Einhard)

Charles was described as temperate in his consumption of both food and drink (in an age and culture where gluttony and heavy drinking were often regularly practised by those who could afford it), and particularly careful when it came to alcohol. He is noted as drinking no more than three cups of wine or beer at a meal, and for punishing drunkenness among his followers.

He often said that religious fasts were bad for the health, and ate in moderation at all times. A typical meal would consist of perhaps four dishes, and his favourite hot roast on a spit, brought directly to his platter from the kitchen. Meals were enlivened by readings or poetry recited or chanted at Charles' command.

Charles was also an active man. He frequently rode and hunted, and enjoyed swimming, at which he excelled. Indeed, his capital city of Aachen (Aix la Chapelle) was partly chosen because of its hot springs, where Charles swam daily in the great bath.

He followed the Frankish manner of dress, hallowed by tradition, and did not wear exotic clothing, even at the height of his power. A typical costume would consist of linen strips wrapped around his feet and calves (stockings and similar wear had not yet been invented), high boots, a linen shirt and underwear, with a woollen overtunic and breeches. The tunic might have a silken decorative border, and in winter a fur coat of ermine would have been worn over the tunic. He also wore a typical bright blue cloak, and always carried a sword with a gilded hilt.

Charlemagne receiving the Oath of Fidelity and Homage from one of his barons in a cameo facsimile from the fourteenth-century Chroniques de Saint Denis.

On state occasions Charles dressed in a tunic and cloak embroidered with gold wire, fastened with gold buckles. He also wore a jewelled crown for such occasions, and a jewelled hilted sword. Yet in everyday dress he was noted for the simplicity of his clothing, and for not setting himself apart from his nobles in appearance.

He was very fond of ancient histories, stories and epics of earlier times and heroes. At this time much of the history was preserved in oral tradition, and there were long Frankish epic poems or cycles of ballads describing the deeds of his predecessors. Charles ordered these epics to be written out – although his son, Louis the Pious, unfortunately had them destroyed when he came to the throne, on account of the pagan content.

Charles also delighted in the works of Saint Augustine, and the *De Civitate Dei* was one of his favourite texts. He was able to read (in a time when many nobles were happily illiterate) and noted for his skill at reading aloud and singing to the harp. He also instructed those around him in these arts, and was far from being just a powerful military ruler. It is, indeed, this rounding and balance of his character and abilities that made Charles such a great ruler. Yet he seemed never quite at ease with his Christianity.

Church, Religion and Morality

For several centuries, Christianity had been the unifying political religion of the Franks. We find in Charles, however, an ambivalent attitude. He frequently attended church, and demanded strict attention and decorous behaviour from his court while at worship. We are told that he could pray in both Frankish and Latin, which was of course the official church language, although this reflects his facility with languages in general rather than any excess of devotion.

Yet he soon divorced his first wife, quite casually, to cement a treaty against his brother Carloman, and certainly paid little or no attention to orthodox Christian morality. On the death of his third wife, Charles lived with no less than three concubines who bore him numerous children. This pagan kingly behaviour (more reminiscent of ancient kingship rights than orthodox Christian behaviour) gave rise to criticism from the Church, but no one dared openly to accuse or chastise such a powerful ruler.

The relaxed morality of Charles himself extended to some, but not all, members of his large family. Two of his daughters lived 'in sin' without any comment from their father, but as soon as Louis the Pious inherited the crown, he banished these sisters to appease the Church and his own sensitive conscience.

Yet Charles was a mighty protector and sponsor of the Church, giving generously, building extensively, and installing clergy, churches and monasteries in his conquered territories. Little wonder that the savage

Saxons regarded Christianity as a Frankish method of suppression and control rather than a true religion in its own right. We might expect such a king to have been beatified upon his death (his ancestor had been St Arnulf) but Charles' indifference to Christian morality prevented this. Indeed, one Wettin of Reichnau, a visionary monk, claimed to have seen Charles in Purgatory, where the purifying flames burned away his lust in preparation for his entry into Heaven.

Charlemagne and his wife, from a ninth-century manuscript.

An impression of St Michael's Chapel at Fulda. This ninth-century, circular section is the only surviving part of the Abbey built by Charlemagne to enforce Christianity upon the pagan Saxons.

In retrospect, we can see Charles as a man of immense energy; we know from chronicles that he slept lightly and that he commenced state work very early in the morning, judging litigants in his private chamber. His astonishing capabilities in the arts and sciences, martial skills and campaigns, statemanship and administration, were simply reflected by his sexual life. Although the Church of the period lamented Charles' sexual vigour and lack of suppressive morality, to the modern imagination it seems remarkable that he could rule a vast empire and still have time to devote to three concubines. A weaker man might have become debauched (as many kings of that time certainly did) yet Charles clearly never allowed his vital energies to weaken his will.

On the negative side and however 'normal' for the period, we must remember that Charles was responsible for a number of massacres during his campaigns; in 782 at Verden, he ordered the slaughter of no less than 4,500 unarmed prisoners. Indeed he was notorious for his policy of 'baptism or death' in respect of the Saxons.

Crowning Victories

On the death of Pepin le Bref, his sons Charles and Carloman immediately had themselves proclaimed as kings by their supporting nobles, and were anointed by their respective bishops. Thus when Charles gained his first crown on 9th October 768, he was far from sole ruler or great emperor. This division of the realm was according to Frankish custom, under which sons shared inheritance of their father's dominions. It had often proven to be a disastrous, or at best weakening, influence upon the stability of the realm, as the inevitable feuds between factions arose from such divisions.

But Pepin had perhaps left his first-born, Charles, superior in power to Carloman, though they ruled jointly from 768 to 772. By the simple expedient of giving Charles control of the military elements of his kingdom, Pepin may have ensured that his elder son would retain greater control. Charles ruled all the Frankish territories which provided the fighting men: from the Main to the Channel, the Austrasian and Neustrian warriors were under his command. He also inherited the western part of Aquitaine, which had been added to the kingdom by conquest in 767, not long before his father's death.

Carloman inherited rulership of Burgundy, Suabian territories on both sides of the Upper Rhine, and the Mediterranean coast from the border of Spain to the Maritime Alps; he also acquired the eastern part of Aquitaine. Thus although his territories were extensive and almost equal to those of his elder brother, the military might and command of the famous Frankish warriors remained mainly with Charles. It was therefore Charles who could dictate policy and law in most respects.

This allocation of power by Pepin was probably based upon his recognition of a feud between Charles and Carloman who, of course, remained unfriendly towards one another after their respective crownings and inheritances. Although Charles was the eldest son, he had been born while his father was still Mayor of the Palace. Carloman, however, had been born after Pepin had been crowned king in his own right and so considered that he held a superior claim to kingship.

As it turned out, the joint reign was short, no more than three years, during which time the feuding brothers were kept in check by the influence of their mother Bertha. Then before an outright war between Charles and Carloman could erupt, the younger brother died, leaving the way open for the development of one of the greatest European emperors in history – but not before earlier triumphs.

Reconquests of Aquitaine 769

As soon as Pepin le Bref was dead, Aquitaine revolted, presumably hoping to take advantage of the disagreement between the old king's heirs and re-establish independence. The ruling Duke Waifer had been

killed in the war with Pepin, but his father, Hunold, came out of
retirement in a monastery to lead the revolt. Support for the aged
warrior extended as far north as Angouleme and seemed to present a
serious threat to Frankish rule in Aquitaine.

Charles, now commander of the military strength of the kingdom,
marched with a large force to subdue Hunold and his supporters. He
invited his brother Carloman to join in the campaign, but they argued
immediately, and Carloman returned to Burgundy, leaving Charles to
continue alone in the reconquest of Aquitaine.

As a result of his leadership, the Frankish army fought through to
Bordeaux and built a huge fortified camp at Fronsac. This camp was so
strong that it remained as a major fortress for the Garonne region for
centuries to follow. The aged Duke Hunold was defeated, and fled to
take refuge with Lupus, Duke of the Gascons. But Lupus shrewdly
submitted to Charles, gave up the offending Aquitaine leader, and was
granted peace. Charles returned in great triumph, indisputable King of
Aquitaine. Hunold was not executed, as we might expect, but returned
to the obscurity of his monastic life. As a final stroke, Charles divided
Aquitaine into countships, the customary Frankish mode of government, placing the command with men from north of the river Loire,
who were entirely his own.

After the reconquest of Aquitaine, Bertha persuaded Charles towards
a reconciliation with his brother. But Charles was already demonstrating
his statesmanship, making treaties with various rulers whose territories
bordered upon those of Carloman. These included Tassilo, Duke of
Bavaria, and Desiderius, King of Lombardy. In these moves Charles was
displaying the combination of martial skill, courage, and shrewd politics
that were to become such a feature of his rapid growth from king into
emperor.

To cement the alliance with Lombardy, Charles married Desiderata,
the daughter of Desiderius. This political marriage was very unpopular
with Pope Stephen III, especially as the papacy had encouraged the
Frankish kings to weaken the power of the Lombards, whose territories

14

bordered upon its own. Charles was requested by Stephen 'not to mix the famous Frankish blood with the perfidious foul leprous Lombard stock – a truly diabolical coupling which no true man could call a marriage . . .'

But Charles was securing his own interests rather than those of the Pope, and proceeded with the marriage despite every threat and protest. After all, Charles never seemed to have held much regard for Christian morality and marriage laws, and certainly was not likely to let papal complaints and rhetoric alter his decisions. Stephen, however, as soon as the marriage with Desiderata was consummated, abandoned all his objections to the 'foul leprous Lombards' and entered into a treaty with Desiderius. Presumably the thought of a combined Frankish and Lombard opposition was too disturbing to bear.

After one year Charles suddenly divorced Desiderata on the grounds that she was barren and weak. He immediately married a Suabian noblewoman called Hildegarde, and so gained a new wife and the unrelenting hatred and opposition of his ex father-in-law.

The Death of Carloman

In 771 it seemed likely that Desiderius would join forces with Carloman against Charles, but in December of that year, the younger Frankish king died. Although Carloman had an infant son, the nobles and bishops of Alamannia and Burgundy immediately travelled to Corbeny-sur-Aisne to do homage to Charles. Suddenly he was ruler of all the Frankish realms.

Opposition to Charles was now centered in Lombardy at the court of Desiderius. Carloman's widow, child, and a small band of supporters were welcomed by the Lombards, who pressed the child's claim to a share of the Frankish kingdom. Despite this counter-claim, Charles now ruled an extensive area: all lands from the Main to the Bay of Biscay, and from the mouth of the Rhone to the mouth of the Rhine, were under his sole dominion. It was a realm controlled by the disciplined military might of the Franks.

Frankish Warfare

There are conflicting theories regarding the methods of combat used by the Franks at the time of Charlemagne. Although Norman horsemen used stirrups, a major invention and development in terms of medieval warfare, it is not certain if the warriors of Charlemagne used them to any great extent. A Frankish stirrup has been discovered by archaeologists, but contemporary records do not confirm that horse charges and similar tactics were widely used.

The soldiers of Charlemagne.

Overseen by evangelist monks, Charlemagne's conquering Franks meet fierce resistance from Saxon tribesmen. The superior might of the Frankish army was often hard pressed in the Saxon wilderness.

The early Franks fought on foot, using spears and single-handed axes, usually with the protection of a shield wall. But by the time of Charlemagne the majority of warriors were on horseback, though it is not clear if they actually *fought* from horseback or if they used the horses simply as rapid transport for traditional Frankish foot soldiers. It is probable that this was a transitional period, in which cavalry techniques and the use of stirrups were being developed, while the earlier form of the armed group and shield wall was still extensively used.

Ornate sword, reputedly Charlemagne's. Frankish swords were the best in Europe; strict legislation was enforced by Charlemagne to prevent exports beyond his realm.

Weaponry and Equipment

Perhaps the most famous weapon of the Franks was the sword: Frankish swords were in great demand across Europe for their balance and temper, and a number of restrictions were issued by Charlemagne controlling their export. The fact that these were generally long swords tends to confirm the use of cavalry. On horseback the long reach of the swordsman is supported by his horse, enabling him to use with great effect a weapon that might be cumbersome on foot.

Infantry carried short swords – the scramasax of Germanic origin. This had a single edge and a thick, heavy blade which could also be used as a bludgeon (the 'flesh cutter' and the 'bone breaker'). Each foot soldier also carried a bow, twelve arrows and a spare bowstring as standard equipment. Finally, they also carried spears. The implication is that the Frankish foot soldier was skilled in all round weaponry, able to fight at a distance and at close quarters. They did not wear much in the way of body protection or helmets (early Frankish shield bosses were at first classified as helmets by early archaeologists).

The horse soldier, however, with his longer sword, wore leather armour in the form of a jerkin or jacket sewn with iron plates reaching to his thighs. He also wore a helmet, and carried the traditional scramasax as a second sword, as well as a spear with a large crosspiece behind the blade, and a round shield.

The typical crosspiece of the Frankish spear implies the use of the weapon from horseback. Without the crosspiece the considerable force of a horse charge would mean that the weapon might be impossible to reclaim or be pulled from the rider's control after striking. From the equipment, we can see that the Frankish horse soldier was in the earliest stages of development into the armed and armoured knight of later centuries.

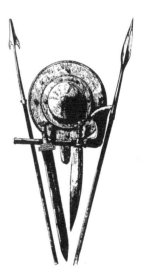

Typical Frankish arms and shields, including the francisca *or war axe.*

The Army

The remarkable achievements of Charlemagne are further emphasized by the fact that he did not have a standing or regular army at any time. All Frankish freemen were required to serve in campaigns when summoned, unpaid and providing their own equipment. We have evidence that booty was divided among the troops as a fairly regular method of

Saracen ambassadors bring Charlemagne a white elephant, complete with exotic trappings. Becoming very attached to this curious animal, he took it on extensive travels until its death.

reward; during the conquest of the Avars, there was even sufficient loot to send gifts to distant Mercia in England. The major divisions went to the nobility, of course, but a Frankish soldier had to fight on command, in the hope that a successful battle or campaign would realise some spoil for himself.

The growing use of cavalry, however, tended to exclude the poorer freemen from fighting in full equipment, and only those with four hides or more of land were required to equip themselves. Mustering was administered by the counts, who were frequently accused of bribery and coercion in the tally of the muster. If anyone failed to attend the muster, heavy fines and punishments could be imposed.

It was the military custom of the Franks to gather the army in spring, and to remain active for three to six months. Under severe campaigning requirements, soldiers could miss both spring planting and autumn harvest, but all campaigning ceased for winter although sieges were sometimes maintained through the winter months by means of entrenched camps and containing earthworks. In many cases the army was mustered as late as May, to allow snow to recede from remote areas, such as the much used Alpine passes.

Soliders were required to bring with them three months' supply of provisions, arms, armour and tools for entrenching and other tasks. Charlemagne was particularly well organised in terms of military mobility and supplies; advance planning was carefully worked out and supplies were often requisitioned in the season before the actual campaign. Herds of cattle and extensive baggage trains followed the troops; the famous romantic exploits of the hero Roland are derived from a historic defence of one such train.

Plundering *en route* was forbidden, probably because it reduced the speed of the army rather than for any ethical reasons. During the Saxon rebellions, however, general looting was allowed as form of punishment for the rebels and as part of a considered plan of devastation. The reward of the soldier, as we have mentioned, was booty from fortified locations taken in battle, and the right to strip the dead of the opposing forces on the battlefield.

Tactics

The planning which made Charlemagne such a successful campaigner was not limited to the organisation of the army's stomach; he employed extensive advance information, usually gathered and considered in the year before each campaign. Every detail of the proposed territory for conquest was examined: population, geography, methods of war, domestic and agricultural patterns of life. This disciplined approach was unusual for the time, and indeed, many later medieval wars were conducted in a far more haphazard manner.

Although an energetic and able warrior, Charlemagne tended to direct

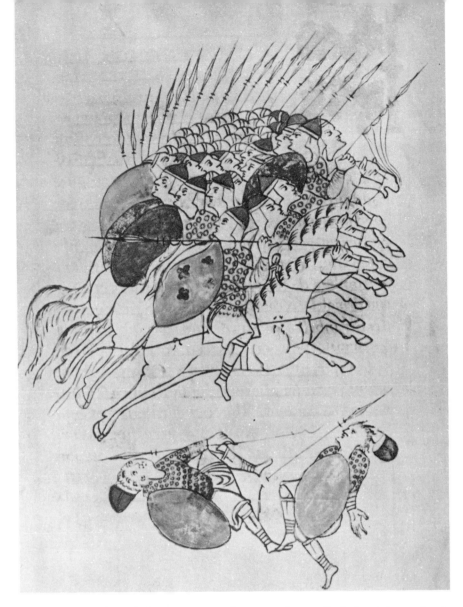

battles rather than fight in person. Once again we find that his methods of command were innovative and successful. His favourite tactic was to divide his forces into two armies, one under himself or a son, and the other under a powerful noble with experience of battle. This two-fold method of invasion, combined with the almost legendary speed of the Frankish forces, tended to keep Charlemagne's opponents confused and uncertain, and when the two forces of the Frankish army reunited, it was usually to deliver a crushing attack upon the targeted opposition.

There is no firm body of evidence of any sophisticated tactics; the foot soldiers were divided into groups who supported the horse soldiers and some men, as we have suggested, rode into battle but fought on foot. The cavalry technique would have been the single mass charge carrying maximum force, with following attacks from foot soldiers. The foot

Armed Frankish horsemen from the Book of Maccabees, *a tenth-century Swiss manuscript from St Gallen. The stylised formation suggests a charging battle tactic. Round shields, chain mail and simple conical helmets are clearly visible.*

were also responsible for entrenchments and for engineering works associated with sieges. Archery seems to have been a minor technique, for men armed with swords and spears and carrying only twelve arrows could hardly be termed 'archers' in the later medieval sense of a specialised separate force of skilled bowmen used as a collective weapon in their right.

First Campaigns

Among the many achievements of Charles, the most obvious is the extent of his military conquests. During his reign he added vast territories to the Frankish kingdom that he had inherited; Lombardy (the traditional enemy of both Franks and papacy), parts of Spain, all of Saxony over a prolonged period of campaigning, and Slavonic regions of the Drave and Elbe.

There is no doubt whatsoever that this expansionism was a deliberate and carefully controlled policy; Charles did not fight defensive or reluctant wars. He greatly amplified the Frankish role, established by his predecessors Charles Martel and Pepin le Bref, as defender of Christianity allied primarily (but not always harmoniously) with the Roman pope rather than the Christian hierarchs and rulers of the Eastern Roman Empire based in Constantinople.

Bronze casting of Thor, the thunder god, who was worshipped extensively in northern Europe at the time of Charlemagne's enforced military evangelism.

This politico-religious stance originated in the necessary defence of Western Europe from the Slavs, Saxons and Saracens, three pagan and savage races who continually sought to invade. But Charles was not merely a defender, and while his ancestors had often been weakened through internal dissent among the Frankish nobility, he had total command and a clear field of action based upon considerable personal and state resources. Thus he actively sought to crush the Slavs and Saxons, and forcibly render them Christian, just as his grandfather Charles Martel (who died in 741) had converted the Frisians and Thuringians.

It was not possible, however, to 'convert' the Saracens; they had a policy of religious expansionism too – seeking to convert all unbelievers to Islam at the point of the sword. Charles sought to expel and chastise the Saracens, keeping them out of his southern territories and securing border areas where they might encroach.

The Lombards were a different matter, for they were a Christian state in Italy. Charles' father, Pepin le Bref, had allied himself with the papacy against Lombardy, but Charles eventually destroyed the Lombards and took the Iron Crown for himself. While this may seem a consolidation of his European realm and role, Charles could not have foreseen that he was

20

to strengthen the future power of the papacy far more than that of his own lineage. When Charles received the (initially) doubtful title of emperor from Pope Leo III on Christmas Day, 800, he set the scene for later claims that the Pope had the power to install, or to depose, the Emperor.

Boundaries of the Realm

At the time of Carloman's death and Charles' succession as sole ruler, the Frankish realm was extensive, but by no means comparable to that later established by Charles himself.

In Germany the northern border was held by the Frisians, and the southern border by the Bavarians. These tribes had been conquered by the Franks and forced into Christianity, but they retained their own kingship or leaders, and were not tightly bound to the Frankish throne in terms of direct government.

Soldier's ornamental helmet from a Frankish grave.

To the east of Frisia were the pagan Saxons, a diffuse and essentially nomadic conglomeration of tribes. Despite 300 years of conflict, the Merovingian kings and their Mayors (who eventually became the Frankish kings in their own right) had found it impossible to subdue the Saxons on any permanent basis. Beyond the Saxons, further east, were the Slavonic tribes of the Sorbs, Abotrites and Wiltzes, also pagan and virtually unknown to the Franks.

To the east of Bavaria were other Slavonic tribes, Czechs, Moravians and Carentanians. Beyond these lay the large realms of the Avars, who were Tartar tribes unified under a ruler known as the Chagan.

21

Between Frisia in the north and Bavaria in the south, the frontier inherited by Charles was held by the Thuringians, who were ruled by Frankish counts. This conquered territory was totally under Charles' control and bordered on the territories of the unconquered Slavonic Sorbs. We will find this system of countships or counties recurring as a basis of Frankish government when we examine the campaigns against the Saxons in detail. The term 'county' for an administrative area is still found in Europe and America today.

To the south-east lay the great mountain chain of the Alps, acting as a barrier (soon to be overcome by Charles) between the Franks and the kingdom of Lombardy. The south-west was bounded by the Pyrenees, beyond which lay the Saracen territories of Spain. At the time of Charles taking his crown, the Saracens were ruled by Abd ar-Rahman the Ommeyad, who had declared his own state independent of the main Abbaside caliphate in 755.

The territories described above were all to feel the military might of the Franks under the remarkable leadership of Charles the Great.

Invasion of Lombardy

King Desiderius, as we have seen, received Carloman's widow Gerberga and her son and supported their claim to the Frankish crown. Lombardy was the first territory to be invaded by Charles, but the Lombard support of the Carloman faction was not the official or even the major reason for the campaign.

The new pope, Hadrian I, repudiated the Lombard alliance made by his predecessor, and demanded territories from Desiderius. He claimed that Ferrara and Faenza had been promised to papal authority in 757 as part of the Exarchate of Ravenna before Desiderius became king and while he was still struggling for the crown with his rival King Ratchis. When this papal claim was made, Charles was busy annexing the territories of the newly deceased Carloman, and seemed unlikely to offer the traditional Frankish support to the pope against the Lombards, based on agreements made by his father Pepin le Bref.

Desiderius responded to the Pope by raising an army and seizing Sinigaglia and Urbino, hitherto papal cities. He then mobilised his full military potential and marched against Rome. Hadrian had already fortified the city and brought in heavy garrisons for defence; he now sent to Charles invoking the agreement between the Franks and the papacy. The Frankish king was expected to enforce the treaty imposed upon the Lombards by his father Pepin, and drive them back to their own territories.

Desiderius, perhaps surprised by this indication that Charles was not so occupied after all, drew back to Viterbo. He then sent a counter-embassy to Charles (in the autumn of 772), explaining that he was not

Armed Frankish horsemen (opposite) as shown in the Golden Psalter. The riders use stirrups and large, supporting saddles, so may be a cavalry unit. They have mail tunics and basic helmets, whilst their banner is a typical 'dragon' or tubular device carried on a long shaft.

ETSYRIAM SOBAL · ETCONVERTIT
IOAB · ETPERCVSSIT EDOMINVAL
LESALINARVM · XII MILIA ·

unlawfully retaining those lands claimed by the Pope on behalf of the Exarchate of Ravenna, as the claim was false.

First Saxon Campaign

Charles, meanwhile, had commenced his first campaign to subdue the Saxons, a task which was not concluded for over 20 years. In the summer of 772 he led an army into middle Saxony, and took hostages from the Engrians. He then destroyed the *Irminsul*, a sacred temple or tree grove worshipped by all Saxony. This religious sanctuary stood near Paderborn, and was a type of national spiritual or magical centre for the widely scattered and nomadic Saxon tribes. Tree worship of this sort was a feature of pagan Germanic, Norse and early Celtic culture, and is still found in myth, legend and folklore in many variant forms. The *Irminsul* was laden with rich sacrificial offerings of wealth, which were plundered by the Franks.

When Charles returned to Austrasia in the autumn, he met the ambassadors of both Hadrian I and Desiderius at Thionville. He supported the Pope, of course, and sent his own embassy to the Lombards demanding that Desiderius remove his forces from the occupied papal cities, and comply further with the Pope's original demands for Ferrara and Faenza. Desiderius refused to obey or accommodate in any way.

By this time winter had arrived, when campaigning usually ceased. We need to remember that, unlike modern warfare, medieval campaigns were seasonal. This seasonal element in warfare persisted as late as the nineteenth century, but in the period of Charles it was often impossible to wage war in the winter, both because of the weather, and because of the basic necessity to harvest crops in autumn for survival of the people. Thus even a standing army (not known in the modern sense at this time) took time off in the winter. Charles' command was based upon support of his nobles, tributary rulers, and their own dependent households and levies; this formidable fighting force was reconvened in the spring of 773 to invade Lombardy.

Return to Lombardy

They marched from Geneva, Charles leading one army over Mont Cenis, while his uncle Bernard led another through the Great St Bernard Pass. The access to Lombardy had already been fortified by Desiderius, with defensive positions in the Alpine gorges at Ivrea and Susa. But a band of Franks climbed over the mountains at Susa and outflanked the Lombards, forcing Desiderius to fall back upon Pavia.

Charles followed his advance band rapidly, and laid siege to Pavia for several months. During this prolonged siege, Desiderius' son Adelchis raised a second Lombard force and took position before Verona. Leaving the blockade of Pavia to a smaller force, Charles marched directly against Lombard the heir Adelchis, taking Verona, Brescia and Bergamo. The unfortunate Lombard prince fled to Constantinople, where he sought help from the Eastern Emperor Constantine Copronymus.

During the prolonged siege of Pavia, with no sign of capitulation from King Desiderius, Charles spent the spring of 774 in Rome. He held meetings there with Hadrian I, and the two leaders, spiritual and temporal, each seeking political self advantage from the other, came to certain understandings.

Charles arrived in Rome, perhaps intentionally, during Holy Week, and celebrated the Easter festivities there in great ostentation and style. His discussions with the Pope led to Charles' confirmation of papal rights over the Exarchate of Ravenna, from Ferrara and Commachio in the north, to Osimo in the south. This grant included those territories or cities disputed between Lombardy and the pope, and basically reaffirmed arrangements made between Charles' father, Pepin le Bref, and Rome. Such a confirmation was to be of great propaganda value to the papacy in addition to its immediate political and financial value; Charles had confirmed that a friendly relationship existed between the great kingdom of the Franks and Rome, and that a pope could make demands upon the Frankish king in full expectation of support and response – perhaps even of obedience.

Submission of Lombardy

By the summer of 774 Pavia was in a state of famine from the long siege, and Desiderius agreed to submit and open the gates on the condition that his life and those of his men would be spared. The Lombard king was exiled to Neustria, and later became a monk in the Abbey of Corbey where he died in his old age. The Lombard royal hoard was divided, as was often the custom, as loot for the Frankish army. Regular pay was not known in those days, and booty was the usual form of reward at the successful conclusion of a campaign.

Prince Adelchis had become a client or patrician at the court of Constantinople; this left Charles free to have himself proclaimed as king in Italy. He ordered all the Lombard dukes to pay homage to him at Pavia, and from that time onwards was known as 'King of the Franks and Lombards, Roman Patrician'. Charles did not make extensive changes in the Lombard government, and retained many of the governors and administrators who had originally served under Desiderius. Some Italian cities were given to Frankish counts in the usual manner, and a garrison was left at Pavia. This moderate policy ensured that Italy would not be a perpetual hotbed of revolt and dissension.

But Arichis of Benevento, son-in-law to Desiderius, refused to do homage to Charles, and in 776 Benevento, Fruili and Spoleto attempted to restore the exiled prince Adelchis. Charles responded immediately, and on this second expedition into Italy, killed the Duke of Fruili in battle. Spoleto was forced to do homage, but Arichis maintained his

Frankish warrior from the time of Charlemagne.

independence in the south until 787 when Charles again entered Italy in person, besiged Salerno, and finally subdued the obstinate duke.

Conquests of Saxony

While Charles was busy fighting the Lombards and making his terms of future agreement with the Pope, the Saxons revolted against Frankish rule and by 775 we find Charles once again marching his armies into Saxony. This was an action that he was to repeat many times before any true subjugation of the Saxons was achieved.

Saxony was divided into four large regions. Closest to the Frankish frontier was Westphalia, whose tribes lived on the Lippe and Ems, and in the region about the Teutoburger Wald. Further east were the Engrians (who had been temporarily subdued in the summer of 772) whose territory included the valley of the Weser, from its mouth to the borders of Hesse. Further east again was Eastphalia, on the Aller, Elbe and Ocker. The Elbe divided the Eastphalians from the Slavonic Abotrites. The fourth Saxon region was that of the Nordalbingians in Holstein, beyond the Elbe, bordering upon Denmark. These were the most savage and primitive of a generally savage race.

Saxony was a wild land in its natural state of heath, marshes and woods. The main hills were in the south, where Saxony included the outriders of the Hartz mountains. There were no towns or large settlements, and very little in the way of static fortification or any points of specific location, though entrenched or mound camps were known. This made conquest almost impossible, as there was nothing to conquer in the customary sense of European or Asiatic warfare.

When the Frankish armies entered Saxony, the Saxons usually hid in the endless forests or untracked marshlands; there they simply waited until the Franks had marched through, and emerged either to harry from behind or continue their nomadic life in another area. There were no roads of any sort, and rapid pursuit of tribal groups was out of the question.

The only viable tactic seemed to be to surround the tribal hosts, forcing them to give hostages and cattle in exchange for leniency. Once the Franks had departed, however, the tribes simply proceeded with revolt and did their best to destroy any remaining Frankish outposts or sympathisers.

When Charles cut down the sacred tree *Irminsul*, he was destroying the one central element of Saxony that all tribes seemed to look to and respect. This one act earned him unfailing hatred and opposition. However Charles saw his conquest of Saxony, it must have seemed to

the Saxons to be a religious war, for they had no firm concepts of centralised government, only tribal nomadic territories, and certainly no need for the town, city and county based Frankish system. The imposition of Christianity upon the greater part of Saxony took Charles until the very end of his long life.

To gain the upper hand Charles had to repeatedly invade and conquer the four Saxon regions; he used drastic techniques of extermination and punishment; he transplanted entire tribes forcibly to weaken any sense of identity and revolution; he built towns, churches and castles wherever possible, and supported large numbers of Christian missionaries to the pagans by force of arms.

In 775 Charles began by invading Westphalia, dispersing the people and taking their large entrenched camp at Sigiburg. He then marched into Engria, reconquered the mid-Saxons, and crossed the river Weser into Eastphalia. It was the Eastphalian tribes who first did homage to Charles, accepting Christianity; they were soon followed by the Engrians, and hostages were taken as security for the oaths made. The Westphalians were more difficult to subdue, however, and Charles ravaged their territory, slaughtering the warriors and people ruthlessly. Upon their submission, the Westphalians were held in check by garrisons at two large Frankish camps, at Eresburg and Sigiburg. Many hostages from the families of tribal chiefs were taken, mainly youths who were deposited in Christian monasteries in Austrasia, Charles'

The Enger Reliquary showing the figures of Christ and the Virgin accompanied by angels and apostles. This gold-covered oak cask was given by Charles to the Saxon chieftain Wittikind as a gift when he finally surrendered and accepted baptism in the year 785.

27

homeland territory. As a result of this first extensive conquest of Saxony, three-quarters of the Saxons did homage to Charles, but not for long.

Second Conquest of Saxony

As might be guessed from the nature of the Saxons and their land, Charles was soon forced to return and re-establish his supremacy. In 776, when the Frankish army set out on the second invasion of Italy to quell the rebellious supporters of Prince Adelchis, the Westphalians and Engrians revolted.

The camp at Eresburg was taken and the garrison put to death, but the camp at Sigiburg held out. When Charles heard this news, and we must remember that even the fastest military courier might take weeks to bring such a message, he returned to Saxony with astonishing speed, taking the Saxons by surprise.

The shock of Charles and his army appearing suddenly when they were supposed to be usefully employed in far distant Italy filled the Saxons with fear, and they sued for peace. The leaders accepted baptism for themselves and their people, and promised to hold their lands as vassals of the Frankish king. Thus Saxony was conquered for a second time.

One chieftain, Wittikind, fled north to take refuge with the Danes, a race hardly known to the Franks at that time, but who would later make inroads into the empire. The garrison at Eresburg was replaced, and Charles ordered the construction of another entrenched camp at Karlstadt. He then remained in Austrasia for the winter, keeping close to the Saxon border, ready for further insurrection.

The following spring Charles called a great council at Paderborn, in the centre of Engria, to confirm that Saxony was now indeed part of the Frankish realm. Many Saxons were baptised and swore oaths to remain loyal, on threat of forfeiture of their lands and freedom.

The great council at Paderborn was also attended by ambassadors from Saracen Spain, with a surprising offer of homage from Soliman Ibn-al-Arabi and Kasmin Ibn-Yussuf. These chiefs held the north-eastern towns of Barcelona, Huseca and Gerona, close to Charles' border. They proposed that they became Frankish vassals in return for protection against the expanding might of Abd-ar-Rahman the Ommeyad, who had taken over virtually the whole of Spain.

Charles, thinking that Saxony was now safely secured, accepted this offer, which effectively pushed his own frontier beyond the Pyrenees. In 778 he led a huge army into Spain.

Invasion of Spain

Charles led an army of Neustrians over the western Pyrenees, while a further force levied from Austrasia, Lombardy and Burgundy, crossed

the eastern Pyrenees. Before Saragossa the two Frankish hosts joined together, and the king received homage from those Saracen chiefs who had invited him into Spain as their protector.

However, Saragossa could not be taken, despite the vast forces set against it and Charles decided to return to Aquitaine, having gained very little other than the defeat of the Basques after storming Pamplona. Neither the Saracen vassals nor the Basque and Navarese vassals were trustworthy, and in 778 while the army was returning across the Pyrenees, Basque warriors attacked the wagon train, capturing considerable amounts of booty and killing three senior members of Charles' government. This was the background to one of the most famous incidents of heroism in early literature, for the pass was Ronscevalles and

The fall of Pamplona, from a detail on Charlemagne's tomb at Aachen. He is seen on his knees, whilst God shatters the wall held by the defending Moslem forces.

29

the dead men were Eggihard the Seneschal, Anselm, Count of the Palace, and Roland, Warden of the Breton Marches. Very little is known historically about Roland, but his fame lives on in the *Chanson de Roland* and legends that arose not long after his heroic death.

Upon reaching Aquitaine after this defeat at the hands of the Basques, Charles was informed that the Saxons had uprisen yet again. Wittikind, who had not sworn fealty to Charles, had returned from his exile in Denmark to arouse his countrymen and a huge Saxon host had attacked the fort at Karlstadt, taking revenge for the destruction of the sacred *Irminsul* and Charles' other ravages of Saxony. Churches were burned, priests and peasants put to death, and the Saxon nationalists (if they may be called such) were further strengthened by the fact that Charles did not muster a Frankish army until the summer of 779.

The by now familiar pattern repeated itself; Westphalia was finally put to fire and sword by the avenging Franks, and the Westphalians were defeated. The Eastphalians and Engrians submitted without giving battle, and Charles retired to consider how he might best keep the Saxons under submission.

Fourth Conquest of Saxony

In the spring of 780, Charles ordered a council or diet at the head of the River Lippe, and initiated a plan for the control of Saxony. The entire land was to be divided into missionary territories, each division under the religious instruction of a group of monks from Austrasia.

This division was aimed at establishing regular bishoprics which combined secular and religious political control; such bishoprics would be part of the state system of government along with minor kingships, dukes, counts and other nobles and officials. Once again, Charles proved the effectiveness of Christianity as a tool of suppression; there seems little doubt that it was the only possible way to control the Saxons. Many thousands of pagans were baptised and Charles himself is recorded as assisting in mass baptism in the rivers Elbe and Ocker in 780.

Between 780 and 782 Saxony seemed to be well under control; even when Charles left the country, no immediate rebellion occurred, and enforced missionary work seemed to be successful. Once again, it was fear of Charles and his military might that converted the Saxons, not love of Christ (who must have seemed to them a very hard, vengeful god indeed).

As a result of this progress, Charles divided Saxony into countships for civil rule, giving office not only to Frankish favourites and able governors, but also to Saxon chieftains. This moderate system of government was frequently adopted by Charles, who early on in his reign had recognised the wisdom of leaving local leaders in place wherever it seemed possible and beneficial to his own aims. A Saxon code of law was published, which dealt firmly with reversions to paganism; any return to the old way of worship was punished by death. Crimes specified were robbing churches, burning instead of burying the dead, deriding Christian services and practices, and sacrificing to Woden. The death penalty could also be applied to those who refused baptism, failed to conform to ecclesiastical disciplines given out by missionary leaders, or who refused to fast in Lent. Fines could also be imposed.

The Massacre of Verden

By 782, in response to this increased formalising and application of militant Christianity, Wittikind returned again from his refuge in pagan Denmark and summoned the northern tribes to revolt. Once again Charles applied superior force, and many of the rebels immediately submitted. But churches had been burnt, priests killed, and proud Saxons had ritually washed off their enforced baptism. Charles resolved upon a severe punishment.

The most active rebel leaders and warriors were brought as captives to Charles on his command; 4,500 men were bound and taken by their countrymen to a camp at Verden on the River Aller. Charles ordered the beheading of the entire company, bound and helpless as they were.

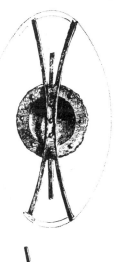

Once again the Saxons showed their spirit, and rose *en masse* to avenge this cruel execution. Even the most obliging and servile tribes took arms against Charles; the matter was now one of a blood feud as well as a religious war. Between 783 and 785 there was continual conflict across Saxony. Charles swept the land twice with his armies, burning and killing wherever he could find victims, but the Saxons held out in the impenetrable forests and marshes, closing in behind the Frankish military movements.

In the winter of 784 Charles and his army remained in Minden in the middle of Saxony, an unusual move designed to weaken the rebels, who were accustomed to 'the great king' leaving their land each winter.

Fifth Conquest of Saxony

In 785 Charles' inflexible attitude and persistent presence finally paid off; the main nationalist leader, Wittikind, sued for peace and was given his life in exchange for his surrender and baptism. When Wittikind and his warriors capitulated, the revolt began to collapse. Charles reinstated his counts, rebuilt his churches, installed new priests, and the Saxons found themselves back under Frankish control.

Between 785 and 792, Frankish rule was consolidated in Saxony. There were four further uprisings between 792 and 804, but these occurred in a Saxony that was already well under control and were readily crushed. In 788 Charles replaced his vassal Tassilo, Duke of Bavaria, with the effective countship system of government. The disloyal Duke, who had frequently been rebellious, was exiled to the

The umbo or boss of a Frankish shield from below and in profile. Early archaeology mistook these for helmets.

31

Neustrian monastery of Jumieges. With this annexation of Bavaria, Charles completed his conquest of the Saxons and the Germans and he now turned his attention to other regions bordering upon his extensive kingdom.

Extending the Kingdom

From around 785 to 814 Charles entered into a second stage of his expansion and conquests. During this period we find him in conflict with races who were very different to the Franks: the Slavs and Avars in the east and the Saracens in the south and west. He also came into conflict with the Empire of the East, an orthodox Christian empire with territories touching upon those of Italy, with many differences and oppositions to papal and Frankish interests.

During the second phase of expansion, Charles allocated authority to his three sons; each had a kingdom under Charles, and was expected to guard the borders against hostile invasion. The eldest son, another Charles, ruled western Neustria, which consisted of Anjou, Maine and Touraine. The second son, named Pepin after his grandfather, ruled Lombardy. Ludovic or Louis, the youngest, ruled Aquitaine.

Thus Louis controlled the frontier with the Saracens in the Pyrenees, Pepin curtailed the Duke of Benevento and defended north-eastern Italy against incursions by the Avars, and Charles the Younger fought against the Bretons of Armorica, who rebelled in 786 and 799 against Frankish rule.

In addition to fixed territories and frontier duties, the sons were also employed by their father on specific campaigns in other territories. Pepin directed campaigns against the Slavs in Bohemia; Louis conducted campaigns in southern Italy, though he was by no means a military leader by nature; and Charles the Younger led forces against the Saxons in his father's name.

It seems to have been Charles' policy to broaden the education and leadership of his sons, and at the same time not to allow them to become too entrenched in their own subkingdoms. In addition to the mobility required of them as deputies in battle for the king, they were also kept in attendance at their father's court at Aachen for long periods of time. It was partly this prudent use of his sons that enabled Charles to expand, control and defend his kingdom upon many fronts at once.

Subjugation of the Slavs
The far north-eastern border of Charles' kingdom joined upon the

Frankish soldiers commit a terrible mass execution of defiant Saxons at Verden. Charlemagne's order of the beheading of 4,500 bound prisoners earned him the Saxon's bitter hatred for many years.

territories of various Slavonic tribes. They were a primitive and tribal people, and do not seem to have been such fierce opponents as the Saxons. The main tribes, as mentioned earlier were the Abotrites, the Sorbs and the Wiltzes, ruled by various chiefs and tribal princes who were not unified in their opposition to the Franks.

Charles crossed the River Elbe in 789 with an army of Franks, Frisians and Saxons. The Saxons were fighting the Slavs as ancestral enemies and so were an excellent choice; furthermore they were increasingly absorbed into Charles' system of government, and would have to guard the borders upon his departure. The Slav opposition collapsed almost immediately, as if the very name of Charles had struck terror into their hearts.

Witzin, King of the Abotrites, and Dragovit, King of the Wiltzes did homage to Charles, paid tribute and gave hostages. More important for the long-term programme of submission was the fact that they agreed to allow Christian missionaries into their lands. The Frankish army secured most of the northern territories, and the Slavs kept their word to Charles. In 795 they aided the Franks against rebellious Saxons, and in 798 the King of the Abotrites actually conquered Nordalbingian rebels, captured their leader and brought him to Charles. Within a decade most of the Slavs were fighting Danish invaders on behalf of the Frankish Empire.

Conflict with the Avars

In 805–6 Charles sent his eldest son against the Czechs of Bohemia. Charles the Younger wasted the region of the Upper Elbe so thoroughly that the Czechs submitted, and agreed to pay tribute to the Franks.

Along the rivers Danube, Raab and Leithe, to the south of Bohemia, Charles' borders were fringed by the Avars. These were a Tartar people who had been traditional enemies of the Lombards and the Eastern Empire at Constantinople for generations. In 788 the Avars invaded the Lombard territory of Fruili and the Duchy of Bavaria, both under Charles' rule. The days of immediate response and speedy marches were over for Charles with such a complex and expanding realm to govern; two years passed before he invaded the Avar lands in retribution.

Charles led an Austrasian and Saxon army personally down the Danube, and wasted Avar territories as far as the River Raab. Simultaneously a huge Lombard army marched through the valley of the Drave into the middle of Pannonia. This host defeated the Avars in battle and stormed their camps. It seemed likely that the Avars would be subjected to Frankish rule, but revolt in Saxony called Charles away. For the following two campaigning seasons Charles subdued Saxons. In fact, he did not personally lead forces against the Avars again.

His son Pepin, aided by Eric of Fruili, now led the campaign in Charles' absence. They captured the Avars royal circular camp and sent

Charlemagne's baggage train is attacked whilst crossing the Alps on one of his campaigns. Massive baggage trains enabled rapid troop movement by the Frankish army without repeated foraging.

great booty to Aachen. There was so much spoil from this Avar stronghold that Charles used it as gifts, and it was some of of this booty that reached the distant King Offa of Mercia, in central Britain.

Eventually the Avars did homage to Charles; their *tuduns* or chieftains came to Aachen and were baptised. In 805 Charles chose one chieftain to reign as his vassal king, and bestowed upon him the ancient title of Chagan, which had originally been that of the independent High King of the Avars. Upon baptism this king took the Christian name of Abraham – perhaps because he hoped to be the father of a long line of kings associated with Frankish power.

To the south of the Avars, the Bavarian and Lombard forces also subdued the Slavs of Drave and Save. Known as Carinthians and Slovenians, these tribes, at one time vassals of the original Avar Chagans, now paid tribute to Charles, though they were not fully absorbed into the Frankish realm or system of government.

The Eastern Empire, Italy and Spain

In Italy, control eventually devolved to Pepin, the second son of Charles. As described, he had to contain the troublesome region of Benevento, but another power also held parts of southern Italy, the Eastern Empire based at Constantinople.

The Diadem Crown of Charlemagne now held in Vienna.

34

Eastern Imperial territories in Italy included Naples, Brindisi and Reggio, with homage from the independent states of Venice and Istria. For much of Charles' reign Constantinople was under the control of relatively ineffectual rulers, and had many internal disputes and factions which made imperial interest in Italy difficult to enforce. Between 780–790 and 797–802, the Empress Irene ruled, a matter which was regarded with much scorn, fear and loathing by the European Church. Then from 802–811 the unsurper Nicephorus I held the throne. This unstable situation did not prevent intense imperial resentment of Charles' growing power.

When Charles was eventually declared Emperor of the West in 800 the Eastern Empire regarded this (perhaps correctly) as usurpation of a title that belonged to Constantinople. To a certain extent the East Romans, as they were still called, were genuine heirs to the original Roman Empire, their capital having been founded by Constantine the Great in 324–340. The Franks, on the other hand, were the heirs of the barbarians who had destroyed the Roman Empire in the West.

As we have seen, Constantinople gave refuge to Prince Adelchis (son of Charles' first father-in-law, Desiderius), who still maintained op-

Charlemagne's stone throne in the Octagon at Aachen Cathedral. Originally, this symbolic seat of power contained holy relics.

35

position to Charles in Italy, albeit from afar. But between 804 and 810, Nicephorus I commanded a series of expeditions against Italy, for Venice had transferred her homage to Charles. Nicephorus' fleet harried the accessible southern coasts in retribution, but made no firm gains. Then when a pro-East Roman party gained control of Venice, allegiance was declared in favour of Nicephorus once again, and peace was made with Charles.

As a result of these disputes, Charles gained possession of a number of Istrian coastal cities which had originally been under the rule of Constantinople. In 812 Nicephorus was succeeded by Michael Rhangabe, who recognised Charles as Emperor of the West, despite much opposition from his own people. It seemed clear that the Franks were a power in Europe that the Eastern Empire did not dare to challenge on a large scale.

Expansion into Spain
As the boundaries of Charles' dominions extended southwards in Italy, he came into conflict with the Saracens, who were widespread in the Mediterranean. When Charles took Corsica and Sardinia, he drove out Saracens who had taken these islands, in turn, from the East Romans. In 799 the Franks took the Balearic Islands, which faced repeated attacks from Saracen fleets, but were held under the government of the Counts of Genoa and Tuscany.

In Spain there was unbroken war with the Saracens. In 785 the Franks advanced over the Pyrenees and took Genoa; internal dissent between rival Moslem factions helped Charles' gradual conquest of Spain, but it was no easy task. The Spanish wars were led by Louis, Charles' third son, now King of Aquitaine. His chief councillor and military leader was William of Toulouse, one of the great Frankish heroes. It seems likely, judging from Louis' later life, that the military effort was mainly conducted by William, for the King of Aquitaine was inclined more to the cloister and altar than the sword and buckler.

Saracen opposition came from two powerful Ommayad kings of Cordova: Abd ar-Rahman (756–788) and Hisham (788–807). As a result of rebellion by their own Moslem vassals, to whom religious unity was less important than political power, these rulers were frequently faced by Frankish armies called in as allies by the rebels. In 795 Charles created the territory of the March of Spain, incorporating those gains made beyond the Pyrenees and including Ausona, Cardona, Gerona and Urgel. In 797 Barcelona, the main Catelonian city, fell to the Franks and the Saracen governor, Zeid, rebelling against his master in Cordova, sought vassalage with the Christians rather than defeat at the hands of a fellow Moslem.

In 799 the Moors retook Barcelona, and King Louis of Aquitaine laid siege to it. It finally fell two years later as a result of famine, having been surrounded by Frankish earthworks and troops who had remained

Decorated hunting horn reputed to have belonged to Charlemagne.

through the winter months. After this second surrender of Barcelona the Moorish population was removed, and the city repopulated with people from Septimania, thus ensuring that further racial and religious ties would not weaken this important stronghold in Spain. Charles now proceeded to push the Frankish border further south.

In 809 Tarragona fell, and in 811 Charles took the important fortress of Tortosa, which controlled the lower part of the river Ebro. From there the Franks crossed over into Valencia, where they did extensive damage. In 812 the third Ommeyad ruler in Cordova, Al-Hakem, sought terms with Charles. It must have seemed clear to him that the Frankish advance could not be stopped by armed opposition, for he ceded to Charles all the territories gained across the Pyrenees. In later years Barcelona and the region to the north formed part of the kingdom of Arragon, and acted as a buffer against Saracen invasions into the rest of Europe.

Final Saxon Campaigns

In 792 the Saxons revolted yet again; this time it took two years of campaigning to suppress the Eastphalians and Nordalbingians involved. It is interesting that Charles' army now consisted in part of Christianised Saxons and Abotrite Slavs.

As late as 804 the northernmost Saxon tribes revolted once more, and on this occasion Charles resorted to deportation as a cure. Ten thousand Nordalbingian families, effectively the whole race, were transported to Gaul, and settled in small colonies among the Neustrians, many as slaves. The depopulated territories were given to Charles' loyal vassal, the King of the Abotrites. This massive forced deportation concluded Charles' conquest of Saxony, for as a chronicler records 'henceforth they abandoned worship of evil spirits, and gave up the wicked customs of their forefathers, received the sacrament of Chrisitan baptism, mingling with the Franks until at last they were reckoned as one race . . .'

Between 804 and 806 Charles placed bishops at Munster, Bremen and Paderborn (in north, west and south Saxony). It was this establishment of bishoprics that finally destroyed Saxon identity, for life began to revolve around centralised locations with the bishoprics generating towns, and the ancient semi-nomadic life was eroded.

Conflict with the Danes

As already described, the Saxon rebel Wittikind fled to the Danes for protection during the second conquest of Saxony in 776. By 808 the Danes were fully aware of the danger of Frankish expansion, and their king, Godfred, built a massive earthwork along his frontier. The *Dannewerk* at the narrowest point of the isthmus of Schleswig, reached from sea to sea, and remained as a strategic position in wars between Danes and Germans until as late as the nineteenth century.

The Danes also began to attack and raid along the Flemish and Frisian coasts, reaching as far south as the mouth of the Seine. They also attacked Charles' Slavonic subjects on the Baltic. King Godfred made extensive forays into Frisia, and subdued the Abotrites and Wiltzes. His tactic was simple: he harried the coastline wherever it was not heavily guarded, and simply withdrew by sea when Frankish opposition appeared. In 810 he even boasted that he might visit Charles in Aachen, as he had already made deep inroads into Frisia. This threat was never to be fulfilled, for Godfred was conveniently murdered, and his successor and nephew, Hemming, made peace with the Franks.

Emperor of the West

Strictly speaking, the original Roman Empire survived only in Constantinople as the 'East Romans', separate from Rome itself in culture, and, for some periods, in interpretation and practice of Christian religion. There had not been an *Augustus* or Western Emperor for centuries, but the concept remained, and papal authority tended to repudiate Constantinople, even without a Western Emperor. When the Empress Irene took the Eastern throne, Rome refused to recognise her authority. The scene was already set for Charles to become a new Western Emperor.

In 800 Pope Leo III was taken prisoner by relatives of his predecessor Hadrian I. They tried to blind him, but he escaped and fled over the Alps to Charles, who was encamped at Paderborn in central Saxony. Charles resolved to travel to Rome to settle the feud, and gave Leo the protection of Frankish warriors to return home in the meantime. Towards the end of the year Charles travelled to Rome himself, and held a synod to investigate the matter. Not surprisingly, Leo was found innocent and his enemies were executed or imprisoned; after a ceremonial oath taking, Leo III was reinstated as Pope.

By this time the festival of Christmas had arrived, and both papal and royal courts joined together to celebrate in St Peter's basilica. At the close of the service, while Charles kneeled in prayer, Leo placed a diadem on the king's head and pronounced: 'God grant life and victory to Charles the Augustus, crowned by God great and pacific Emperor of the Romans'. This theatrical cry was taken up by the assembled Franks and Romans, and all present, including the pope, prostrated themselves before Charles in the ancient manner reserved for Emperor of Rome.

We might think, in retrospect, that it was a set piece of rather obvious connivance; Charles ruled Europe in any case, and his elevation to emperor seemed to solve the problem of the notorious Empress Irene in Constantinople. But there were no legal precedents for a barbarian emperor, and certainly no precedents for the imperial power being bestowed by a pope.

Charles stated that he did not know what was to take place, and would not have entered St Peter's basilica if he had known. Like other monarchs through history, Charles took the course of letting another take the most major step on his behalf; if it went wrong he could repudiate it, if it went well then it was obviously a wise action for all. There was little doubt that the crowning, vexed with political and religious implications and problems as it was, had popular approval.

The name of emperor had ceased among the Greeks (of Constantinople) for they were enduring the reign of a woman, wherefore it seemed good both to Leo the apostolic Pope, and to the holy fathers in council with him, and to all Christian men, that they should hail Charles king of the Franks as emperor. For he held Rome itself, where the ancient Caesars had always dwelt, and all those other possessions of his own in Italy,

These fourteenth-century miniatures from the Chroniques de Saint Denis *depict (left) Charlemagne's coronation by Pope Leo III and (right) 'Charlemagne's Vision'.*

39

Gaul, and Germany. Wherefore as God had granted him all these dominions, it seemed just to them that he should accept the imperial title also, when it was offered to him by the consent of all Christendom.

(Chronicle of Lauresheim)

The Pope implied that apostolic or divine inspiration had led to the crowning, Charles was therefore 'crowned by God'. This side-stepped the legal aspects of the coronation, for the combined nations of Europe might have chosen to elect an emperor by some other means – though undoubtedly this person would have been Charles. In the long term the crowning of Charles by Leo III led to an increasing papal claim to power over the imperial ruler of the West, but short-term benefits to Charles were clear. In addition to being elected King of the Franks, and overlord of vast territories in Europe, Charles was now divinely crowned. He did not hesitate to emphasise his authority in religious matters, which were already such an integral part of his system of government.

Imperial Rule

After the dramatic crowning of Charles – the first and last time that a pope paid homage to the new Emperors of the West – came a period of reinforcement of his new status. Charles made his subjects swear a new form of allegiance to him as emperor, the vow being administered to all people over the age of twelve:

His vow of homage was not merely a promise to be true to the emperor and to serve him against his enemies, but a promise to live in obedience to God and His law according to the best of each man's strength and understanding. It was a vow to abstain from theft and oppression and injustice, no less than from heathen practices and witchcraft; a vow to do no wrong to the Churches of God, nor to injure widows and orphans, of whom the emperor is the chosen protector and guardian.

Thus law, religion and mortality were all bound up in the imperial title and role, and any offence against the Emperor and his law was an offence directly against God. It is from this carefully defined power base that the concept of the Holy Roman Empire began – a concept that was to have a profound effect upon European history.

The extensive military conquests had been turned, through one ritual act in Rome, into a spiritual empire, with church and state unified under the control of a reigning emperor. The ultimate image was perhaps one of benevolent religious despotism, with the ruler under divine blessing taking care of all members of his realm. It was never realised as such, of course, and the conflict for supremacy between popes and kings took centuries to resolve. Initially, the effect of Leo III crowning Charles was to greatly strengthen papal power, though this was not fully apparent until after Charles' death.

Division of the Empire

In 806 Charles declared the future division of his empire. Upon his death the title of Emperor, the Frankish territories of Austrasia and Neustria, plus Saxony, Burgundy and Thuringia, would go to his eldest son Charles. His second son Pepin would rule Italy, Bavaria and eastern Suabia. Louis (later to be known as 'the Pious') would rule the Spanish March, Aquitaine and Provence. Such division among sons was traditional to the Franks, and comprised an important part of their ancient, mainly unwritten, code of laws.

However, both Charles the Younger and Pepin died within one year of each other, the eldest in 811, his brother in 810. Suddenly Louis was heir to a vast realm that excluded only Italy, which was to be a vassal kingdom for Pepin's son Bernard.

The Death of Charles

Charles died on the 28th January 814, after complications following a winter cold. He was buried in the cathedral at Aachen, in a sacrophagus taken from an ancient Roman site somewhere in Italy. A golden shrine was placed over his tomb, with an image of Charles and the simple inscription:

Sub hoc conditorio situm est corpus Karoli Magni et orthodoxi imperatoris, qui regnum francorum nobiliter apliavit, et per annos xlvii feliciter rexit.

Within this tomb is laid the body of the Christian Emperor Charlemagne, who guided the kingdom of the Franks with distinction and ruled it with success for 47 years.

(trans: Colin Stockford)

The Charlemagne Legacy

The achievements of Charles the Great were comprehensive: in addition to advances in religion, law and military rule during his reign, he worked extensively to develop learning within his empire. However, one must realise that religion, law, rule and learning were fused together in the consciousness of the eighth and ninth centuries. Charles worked very hard indeed to strengthen this fusion, under the single role of emperor, as leader of all human endeavour and development.

Cultural Achievements

Charles made serious efforts to develop the learning and culture of his court and society. He summoned scholars and men of wisdom from all over the known world, his main personal tutor and mentor being Alcuin of Northumberland from England. Alcuin taught Charles dialectic and rhetoric, while grammar was taught by Peter of Pisa. In encouraging scholars to attend his palace, Charlemagne allowed a freedom of speech which would have been unthinkable from other men. Alcuin argued openly with him over subjects such as the enforced baptism of Saxons. We may see in this encouragement of scholars not only an attempt to improve the status of the realm, but a genuine curiosity for learning on the part of Charles himself. These scholars taught the 'liberal arts' which Charles sought to learn and instill in his court; they do not correspond to our modern subjects of the same name, but have a wider philosophical and metaphysical basis.

Like most rulers in the Dark Ages and the later Medieval and Renaissance periods, Charles paid attention to the patterns of the stars and planets; he studied the astronomy of the time, which was unified with astrology and philosophy based upon the Four Elements (Air, Fire, Water, Earth). He even devised new German names for the twelve winds and the twelve months of the year, showing a depth of interest and love of order that far exceeds mere military might and cunning. It was this vision of order that held his vast empire together and on his death the entire vision collapsed, and the realm rapidly fell into decay and disunity.

In a practical sense, he encouraged and demanded higher standards of literacy from his churchmen and governors, and issued various proclamations condemning their ignorance of Latin. Schools were started in the monasteries, for Charles proclaimed that 'Men of God should not only live by the rule and dwell in holy conversation, but should devote themselves to literary meditations, each according to his ability, that they may be able to give themselves to the duty of teaching others.'

He even learned to write himself, an art normally left to professional scribes and often despised by members of the militaristic nobility. His signature is preserved to this day on documents. Unfortunately, he was already an adult when he took up writing, and did not become fluent. Nevertheless we are told that he kept tablets or notebooks under his pillow, and would practise his letters from time to time. It is worth considering that hands long formed to the sword, reins, shield and other military accoutrements become stiffened and calloused and it may be that the use of a small stylus or quill was physically difficult for Charles; we can be in no doubt about his energy and intelligence.

Charles also concerned himself with building, and actually helped to design his major cathedral at Aachen, part of which remains today. In the construction marble was brought from Ravenna and Rome, probably taken from earlier Roman works, and bronze rails and doors were cast, with many golden and silver lamps. Church building was also a notable aspect of Charles' government.

Under Charles, the monasteries developed as centres of learning, but he also instigated a programme of reforms of literature, particularly in preservation and copying. Under his instructions, many classical texts were recopied from worn out manuscripts; monasteries were encouraged to make multiple copies of their libraries, and to exchange texts with one another.

Aachen Cathedral (opposite) as it appears today is built around Charlemagne's original chapel and the city still bears the French name of Aix-la-Chapelle.

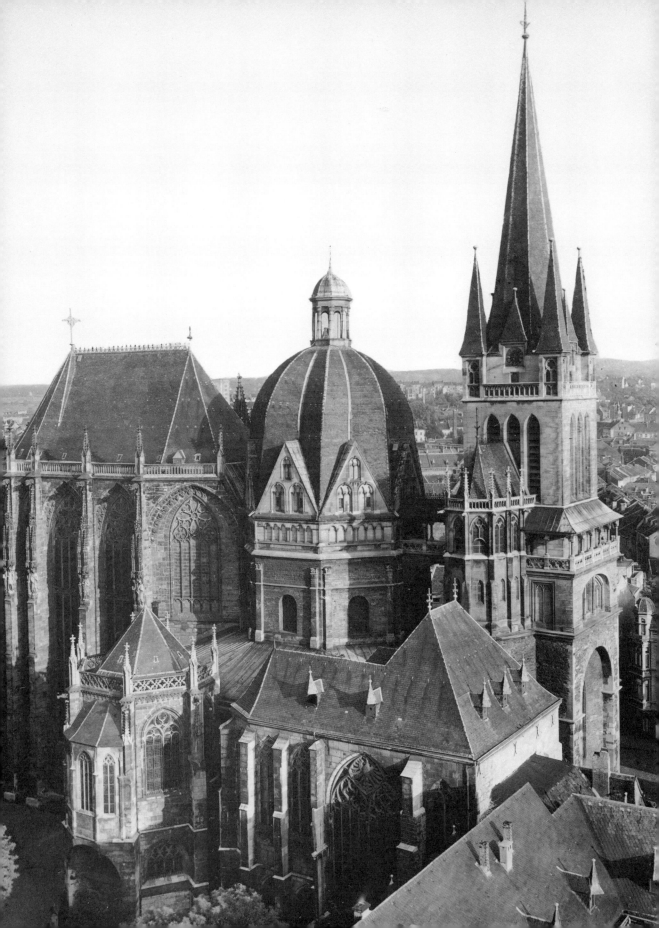

The conquest of Jerusalem as shown in the fifteenth-century Chroniques de Charlemagne.

Charles discovered that there were many variant readings of the Testaments, due to the ignorance of copyists. One of his great scholars, Paul the Deacon, was given the task of preparing a new lectionary (list of lessons for reading), drawn from the best selected texts. This definitive version was to be used in all churches throughout the realm. Traditional epics taken from Frankish oral poetry also commanded Charles' interest, and he had several of these copied out into formal texts. Grammars of Latin and German were assembled by scholars, plus biographies (which formed a major part of medieval literature) and works of history.

Charles' reign was a major turning point in the development of literary records; prior to his time, records were vague and often confusing. Oral tradition played a major role in education, and we we should remember that many of Charles' legal documents were merely written reminders which related to verbal laws, decisions, commands and traditions.

But his rejuvenation of religious and, to a lesser extent, secular, texts and libraries was the first major effort at establishing a corpus of learning in the West on the part of a king since the collapse of the original Roman state. Even styles of handwriting were improved radically, giving clear texts and defined forms.

The main gathering of scholars was at Charles' court, and it seems clear that there was a conscious attempt to restore classical glories, even though much of this did not percolate far beyond the royal circle of intimates. Charles was known as 'King David', and Alcuin as 'Flaccus', while other scholars took the names of Homer, Mopsus and other classical writers. This use of nicknames may seem rather contrived to the modern mind, but allegory, riddling, connective names and patterns, were an integral part of the literature, consciousness and style of the period. Scholars such as Alcuin composed verses with many hidden references or acrostic patterns, and while they may seem trivial today, they represented a quest for pattern, meaning and subtle order, and were not mere exercises in wittiness.

Charles also patronised music and encouraged Italian masters to teach Gregorian chant to the wild choristers of the Frankish and Saxon realms. Art also began to take a distinctive style and many surviving examples combine elements of subtlety, barbaric splendour and beauty. In Aachen, Charles built not only a formal palace, but a huge basilica, some of which was incorporated into what is now the present cathedral.

Depiction of the legendary coronation of Charles in Jerusalem, an example of religiously inspired fiction which also appears in the Chroniques de Charlemagne.

Permanence of Legend

Palaces were constructed in the ancient Austrasian royal centres, and Charles instigated the first major bridge building for centuries, with a structure 500 metres long at Mainz. Although this bridge was destroyed by fire on 813 and not restored, part of another immense feat of engineering remains today in the abandoned canal intended to join the Rhine and Danube.

So great were such feats, and so very great was Charles, that countless legends sprung up around him, and his rule began to be thought of as a golden age. Both the Germans and the French claim him as a hero, and in this sense the Emperor becomes more than a mortal ruler. Like King Arthur of the Britons, Charles the Great, *Caroli Magni*, changed from being a historical person into a legendary ideal – the great ruler who set the world aright, and encouraged men and women to live by a fusion of spiritual and material principles.

Unlike many of his time, Charlemagne had the skill of writing, as in his imperial signature on a document dated 775.

Bibliography

Buckler, F.W. *Harun 'il Rashid and Charles the Great* Cambridge, Mass, 1931.

Bullough, D. *The Age of Charlemagne*, London and New York, 1965.

Fichtenau, H. *The Carolingian Empire* London and New York, 1954.

Heer, F. *Charlemagne and his World* Weidenfeld & Nicolson, London, 1975.

Lamb, H.A. *Charlemagne* London, 1962.

Montgomery Watt, W. *A History of Islamic Spain* Edinburgh, 1965.

Owen, D.D.R. *The Legend of Roland* London and New York, 1973.

Riche, P. *Daily Life in the World of Charlemagne* Liverpool, 1978.

Thompson, A.E. *The Early Germans* Oxford, 1965.

Thorpe, L. (trans). *Einhard and Notker the Stammerer: Two Lives of Charlemagne* Penguin, London, 1969.

GENEALOGY OF CHARACTERS

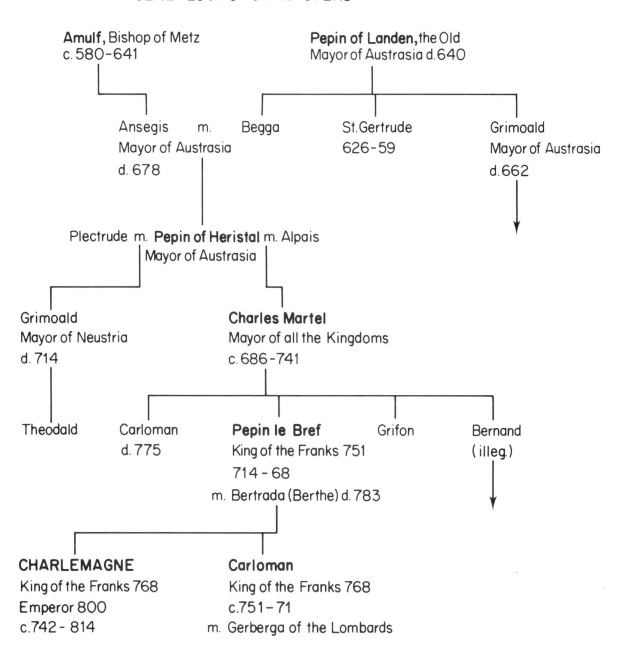

Index

Page numbers in *italics* refer to illustrations.

Illustrations

Colour plates by James Field
Line illustrations by Chesca Potter
Maps and diagrams by Chartwell Illustrators

Photographs and other illustrations courtesy of: Bibliothek des Rijksuniversiteit Leiden/Weidenfeld & Nicolson Archive (page 19); Bildarchiv Foto Marburg/Weidenfeld & Nicolson Archive (pages 35 and 43); Mediatheque Municipale Cambrai/Weidenfeld & Nicolson Archive (page 21); Peter Newark's Historical Pictures (pages 4, 8, 9, 11, 25, 34, 39, 44, 45 and 46); Stadtsbildstelle Aachen/Weidenfeld & Nicolson Archive (page 6); Stiftsbibliothek St Gallen/Weidenfeld & Nicolson Archive (pages 15 and 23).